MAORI ORIGINS
FROM ASIA TO AOTEAROA

Nigel Prickett

Photographs by Krzysztof Pfeiffer

David Bateman

In association with

Auckland **Museum**
Te Papa Whakahiku

MAORI ORIGINS
From Asia to Aotearoa

In the history of New Zealand there is no more interesting or significant subject than the first human settlement of these islands. Who were the first people? Where did they come from – and when? How did they get here? What was their language, and what were the beliefs and way of life they brought with them? How did they set about making a new way of life here? All these questions have for long been subject to research and speculation.

Except for much smaller islands, New Zealand is the most isolated land in the world, being 1800 km from Australia, which is our nearest continental neighbour, 9000 km from South America, and 2500 km from Antarctica. North is the vast Pacific Ocean with its numerous small islands and island groups. Because of its remoteness, New Zealand was the last substantial land-mass in the world to be discovered and settled by humans, other than the Antarctic continent.

It must be stated at the outset that New Zealand's first settlers were the ancestors of the Maori people. These people were, of course, not Maori when they first arrived, since at that time their culture and way of life were the same as that of the people they left behind in their tropical Pacific homeland. The particular character of Maori people and culture grew out of the relationship between their Polynesian inheritance and the unique environment and land they made their home.

Recent research has greatly increased our knowledge regarding the origin of the first New Zealanders. This applies to the coming of Maori ancestors from their immediate homeland in East Polynesia, as well as to the more remote Pacific and Southeast Asian origin of Polynesian people as a whole. The first discovery and settlement of islands throughout the Pacific Ocean is one of the remarkable stories of human history.

Maori themselves have always known where they came from, with the different tribes having accounts of ancestors arriving in ocean-going canoes from a place called 'Hawaiiki'. The whereabouts of Hawaiiki is indicated by the whakatauki, or proverb: 'E kore au e ngaro; te kakano i ruia mai i Rangiatea' – 'I shall never be lost, for I am a seed sown from Rangiatea'. Rangiatea is the Maori pronunciation of 'Ra'iatea', one of the Society Islands, 200 km west of Tahiti.

There is no doubt that Maori ancestors came to New Zealand from somewhere in the Society Islands or central East Polynesia in general – if not necessarily from Ra'iatea itself. But the island was an important centre for religious observances before the arrival of Christianity in the early 19th century; and is notable for its ancient ceremonial stone platforms, or 'marae'. It is not surprising that such a significant island in the religious and cultural landscape of East Polynesia is the one recalled in the whakatauki quoted above.

Out of Asia

Following his visit to New Zealand with Cook in 1769-70, the scientist Joseph Banks wrote of Maori people he had met:

"From the similarity of customs, the still greater of Traditions and the almost identical sameness of Language between these people and those of the Islands in the South Sea there remains little doubt that they came originaly from the same source: but where that Source is future experience may teach us, at Present I can say no more than that I firmly believe that it is to the Westward and by no means to the East."

This accurate summary of the origins of Maori, and of all Polynesian people, remains remarkably unchanged today. Later, Banks visited Java and other places in Southeast Asia, which caused him to consider the similarity of languages there and those spoken in the 'South Seas' – that is, Polynesia. He writes that he would happily have speculated on the historical connection between two places so far apart, but for a disconcerting discovery: he met in Java a man from Madagascar, whose language also was similar to those of Southeast Asia and the Pacific.

Today it is understood how this came about. The major languages of island Southeast Asia and Malaysia, many Pacific languages, and the Malagasy language of Madagascar, all belong to the Malayo-Polynesian branch of the ancient Austronesian language family, which arrived in the Southeast Asian region between four and five thousand years ago. Since then, people have taken Malayo-Polynesian languages with them east into the Pacific

Origins of the Maori language

Maori belongs to the Austronesian family of languages, which can be traced back to the region of south China and Taiwan 5-6000 years ago. A family tree shows the historical relationships of Austronesian languages, following only the line to Maori and other modern Polynesian languages. Older languages shown are ancestral, and are no longer spoken. Dates are approximate.

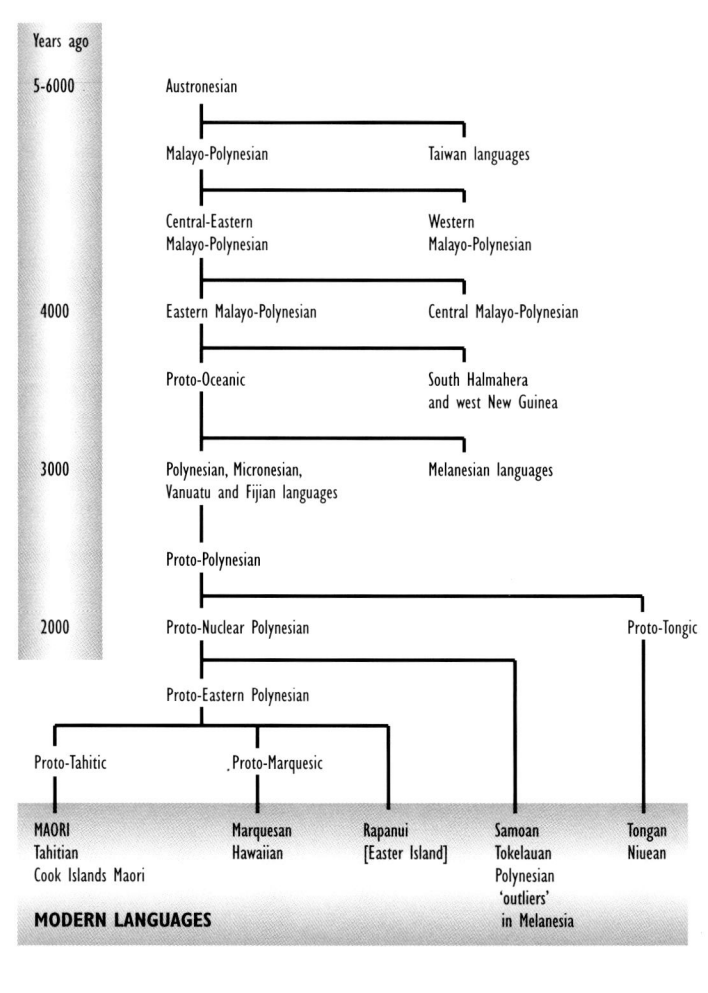

and west to Madagascar. Polynesian languages, including Maori, belong to the Malayo-Polynesian language family.

Just where early Austronesian was first spoken has been subject to considerable research. The linguist Robert Blust points out that, based on evidence now available, the most likely homeland is Taiwan, although it was not necessarily confined to that island. Older linguistic relationships are traced to the Asian mainland in the region of southern China and modern neighbouring states.

At least six primary branches of the Austronesian language family are represented among the 14 remaining native languages of Taiwan. All other Austronesian languages, totalling 1000 or more, fall into a single sub-group termed 'Malayo-Polynesian'. Primary branches reflect the earliest divisions of a language family. Languages spoken today reflect the most recent divisions. The linguistic evidence points to Taiwan being significant in the history of Maori and other Polynesian languages.

The significance of Taiwan is also suggested by archaeology. As we shall see, important aspects of Polynesian cultures are derived from the neolithic culture of Southeast Asia. 'Neolithic' simply means 'new stone' age, referring to the use of polished stone tools; but the word has a wider reference to other cultural attributes as well, such as the use of pottery and cultivation of food plants. The oldest sites in which this early Southeast Asian culture has been identified are found on Taiwan, dating from *ca* 3000 BC. As with the ancient Austronesian language of Taiwan, there are also links to mainland Asian cultures.

Decorated pottery in the northern Philippines island of Luzon dating from *ca* 2500 BC is likely to relate to the earlier Taiwan material, and indicates the movement of these ancient Austronesian speaking peoples into the vast archipelago of Southeast Asia. From there the route may have been south through the Philippines and the Maluku group of Indonesia. By about 1500 BC the maritime people, by then speaking a Malayo-Polynesian language – or languages – descended from Austronesian, and with a 'cultural complex' which is increasingly well-defined by archaeologists, reached the island of Halmahera west of New Guinea.

A 'cultural complex' may be defined as all the archaeological evidence of artefacts, technology, food production, settlement arrangements and other aspects of human culture, which are commonly found together, and thus likely to relate to a particular people or group.

A whalebone disc pendant from the Caroline Islands in Micronesia is like others made of split whale teeth in Fiji or serpentine rock in early Maori culture. Similarities in material culture tell of the shared inheritance of Pacific peoples. Ht 140 mm. (Auckland Museum 15873)

Archaeologists have identified a Southeast Asian neolithic culture dating from about 4000 years ago, which almost certainly is associated with the ancient sea-faring Malayo-Polynesian speakers. It includes pottery, polished stone or tridacna (giant clam) shell adzes, and an economy based on agriculture (including rice and root crops) and the domesticated pig, dog and chicken. Also found are stone hoes and 'reaping knives', bark cloth beaters, clay spindle whorls and ornaments and fishhooks made of shell. Many of these items were later taken into the Pacific in the eastward expansion of Malayo-Polynesian speaking people.

The cultivated food plants, taro, breadfruit, yam, banana and coconut are all found in the wild in Southeast Asia, and, in some cases, New Guinea as well. Words now used for them throughout the Pacific can be traced back to the Malayo-Polynesian language spoken in Southeast Asia 4000 years ago. An example is the word for yam, which in Maori is uwhi or uhi, in Malay – ubi, and in Malagasy – uwi. Domesticated pigs, dogs and chickens also accompanied people throughout the Pacific – but not everywhere, as we shall see.

The multitude of islands and water crossings of Southeast Asia provided a nursery unequalled in the world for the development of sea-going watercraft and a culture of sea-faring. We know that early Malayo-Polynesian speakers were seafarers, from their mobility, and from the shared words relating to seafaring and watercraft, found wherever descendant languages are spoken today. The Maori 'waka' (canoe) and 'ra' (sail), and Malay 'wangka' and 'layar', have the same origin in the ancient Malayo-Polynesian language of Southeast Asia.

That people from Southeast Asia were so successful in expanding over an enormous area of the globe relates directly to their maritime skills and in particular their fast, sea-worthy sailing canoes. From these beginnings were later to develop the knowledge, skill and technology which enabled Pacific people confidently to sail enormous distances over the world's greatest ocean.

The 'Lapita people'

Malayo-Polynesian speakers make their first appearance in the western Pacific as much as 3500 years ago, in the region of the Bismarck Archipelago, east of New Guinea. Their arrival is marked by the sudden appearance of a distinctive decorated pottery with no antecedents in the region, but which has marked similarities to older Southeast Asian ceramic styles.

Other people had been living in the region for as much as 40,000 years, their movement into the area probably aided by the lower sea levels of the Pleistocene Period. This meant that water gaps between islands were not as great as today; in some cases, today's islands were joined by dry land. The newcomers from Southeast Asia, on the other hand, moved rapidly along the seaways, where their ancient settlements are found on coasts and small offshore islets.

There is, of course, no direct evidence of the language spoken by these people; rather, the argument is made from the indirect evidence of artefacts and subsistence economy found by archaeologists. These make up a culture complex which has strong parallels back to older sites in Southeast Asia, and eastwards into the Pacific where today's languages are descended from the Malayo-Polynesian branch of the Austronesian language family.

The people who created these settlement sites in all likelihood spoke a branch of Malayo-Polynesian known as 'Proto-Oceanic', which can be seen on the family tree on page 4. Proto-Oceanic was ancestral to Malayo-Polynesian languages of east New Guinea, the Solomon Islands, Vanuatu, New Caledonia, Fiji, Polynesia and most of Micronesia (but not all of Micronesia, since some islands closest to Southeast Asia were settled directly from the west, and not by way of Melanesia).

The culture complex relating to early Malayo-Polynesian speakers of the western Pacific has been termed 'Lapita' after a place in New Caledonia where a striking form of decorated pottery was found in the early 1950s by archaeologist E.W. Gifford. Gifford saw the similarity of New Caledonian pottery to earlier finds at Watom (New Britain), Tonga and Fiji, and also from Sulawesi in Indonesia, and he used the then new technique of radiocarbon dating to show that the pottery was nearly 3000 years old.

The pottery was much older than was thought likely by many researchers at the time. Also surprising was proof that at this early date, people of similar culture lived in both Melanesia and Polynesia. It had long been thought that the distinctive people and cultures of the two regions indicated very different histories. So different, that distinguished Maori anthropologist Te Rangi Hiroa (Sir Peter Buck) argued for Polynesian ancestors coming into the

A human face looks out from a 3000-year-old Lapita sherd from Nenumbo in the Santa Cruz group, south-east of the Solomon Islands. (Department of Anthropology, University of Auckland)

Decorative motifs on 3000-year-old Lapita pots can be seen on modern Pacific tapa. Samoa; 1550 x 1330 mm. (Auckland Museum 52312)

Pacific via the islands of Micronesia, and not by way of Melanesia at all.

The most distinctive marker of Lapita culture is the decorated and undecorated pottery, which is remarkably alike from the Bismarck Archipelago 4500 km east to the islands of Samoa and Tonga. Complete pots are not found, but broken sherds enable archaeologists to reconstruct the ancient vessel forms. Lapita potters did not use a wheel, but built up their vessels by slabs of clay, or coiling. Firing was carried out at a relatively low temperature, probably on an open fire as Melanesian potters use today.

Although the finely decorated wares are best known, in all Lapita sites most finds are of undecorated wares. There is also a shift over time from decorated wares to undecorated plain pottery. Decoration is noted for its repeated motifs, formed by toothed implements in the soft clay prior to firing, to achieve what is known as 'dentate stamping'. Outstanding among Lapita decoration are stylised representations of the human face. Archaeologist Roger Green has pointed to an interesting link between ancient Lapita design and motifs, and modern Pacific tapa and tattoo patterns.

In a 1997 book, *The Lapita Peoples*, Patrick Kirch lists other characteristics of the Lapita cultural complex. Among them are adzes in stone and shell, shell armbands, pendants, beads, rings and fishhooks, and settlements featuring houses on stilts over water. The economic base is provided by fishing, horticulture based on root and tree crops, and animal husbandry of pigs, dogs and chickens. The people who lived this culture have been termed the 'Lapita people'. Parallels are obvious with the older neolithic culture of Southeast Asia outlined above.

Among features of Lapita culture is the extraordinary mobility of the ancient people who travelled the seas of the western Pacific. This is illustrated by archaeological finds of obsidian ('volcanic glass'), from Talasea on the northern coast of the island of New Britain. Obsidian was valued for knives, made by striking sharp-edged chips off blocks of stone. Differing chemical compositions enable material from the various sources to be identified. For hundreds of years Talasea obsidian was transported 2000 km south-east to ancient settlements in the Santa Cruz Islands. A few pieces even reached Fiji.

Throughout the Bismarck Archipelago and Solomon Islands, contacts between the 'Lapita' newcomers and earlier Melanesian populations are reflected in genetic mixing and linguistic and other cultural borrowing. Not surprisingly, Austronesian-speaking communities remaining in Melanesia to this day are the most profoundly changed by more than three millennia of interaction with other people who live in the region.

People of most Micronesian islands of the western Pacific are descended from Proto-Oceanic speakers who sailed from the Melanesian region *ca* 2000 years ago, and thus reflect more than a thousand years of interaction with Melanesian populations. Least affected, but affected nonetheless, were Polynesian ancestors who, only a short time after their first arrival in Melanesia, crossed the ocean to the relative isolation of the island groups of Fiji, Tonga and Samoa.

Into the unknown

In the story of Polynesian – and Maori – origins an important distinction is to be made between Near and Remote Oceania. 'Near Oceania' comprises all those islands and seas which lie between the so-called 'Wallace Line' (see map pages 16-17) and the south-east end of the Solomon Islands.

Yams, which originate in Southeast Asia, grow on a steep slope above a village on Merelava, Banks Islands, Vanuatu. The islands were first settled about 3000 years ago, during the rapid expansion of Lapita people south and east of the Solomon Islands. (J.W. Beattie, 1906, Auckland Museum 5712)

The line commemorating the 19th-century British biogeographer, Alfred Wallace, separates the rich flora and fauna of Southeast Asia from the relatively impoverished biota to the east. The division is a natural one, falling where deep intervening seas prevented any land bridge throughout the great sea-level fluctuations of the Pleistocene era, and hence allowing relatively few movements of Asian plants and animals.

Beyond the Wallace Line, Near Oceania includes New Guinea and Australia (joined together in an ancient continent called 'Sahulland' when sea levels were low), the Philippines, Sulawesi and islands to the east, and the Bismarck Archipelago and Solomon Islands. The region is dominated by the continent of Australia, and by many large high islands. Few islands are out of sight of the nearest neighbour or neighbours, thus demanding no great seafaring skill in their settlement 40,000 years ago or more.

Eastwards of the Solomon Islands, 'Remote Oceania' is made up of immense distances and tiny islands. Exceptions to the latter are New Zealand's two main islands, each of them bigger than all other

Pottery has been made in Fiji since it was first discovered and settled by Lapita people 3000 years ago. Saqamoli (drinking vessel), Sir George Grey collection, Auckland Museum; Ht 250 mm. (407G)

Jade mace, New Caledonia. Only 1500 km from North Cape, New Zealand, New Caledonia was settled 3000 years ago. 450 mm. (Auckland Museum 23660)

islands of the region together. The fall-off in plant and animal species east of the Wallace Line has already been mentioned; in Remote Oceania there are vastly fewer species again. Native land mammals are completely absent, except for bats which were able to reach distant islands through the power of flight.

Current archaeological knowledge indicates that there was no human settlement in Remote Oceania before the arrival of Lapita people in the western Pacific. Beyond San Cristobal at the southeast end of the Solomons chain was a 350-km water gap to the Santa Cruz group, waiting for a people with the skills and technology to make the crossing.

The first settlement of the islands of Remote Oceania took place within a few hundred years of the arrival of Austronesian speakers in the so-called 'Lapita homeland' of the Bismarck Archipelago. It demanded the crossing of a number of major water gaps, to previously unknown islands. The biggest ocean gap, to Fiji, was at least 800 km from Vanuatu, and possibly a great deal more, depending on the point of departure.

By 1100 BC Lapita people reached the Santa Cruz Islands. The first settlement of Vanuatu and New Caledonia also may have been before 1000 BC. Radiocarbon dates of 1200 BC have been reported from early sites in Fiji, although a recent review suggests first settlement no earlier than 900 BC, which fits better with what we know of early settlement in Santa Cruz and Vanuatu. The first settlement of Tonga and Samoa may also prove later than long accepted dates as early as 1000 BC.

Precise dating of the initial settlement of Vanuatu and New Caledonia, and Fiji, Tonga and Samoa will tell us whether the process was progressive or virtually simultaneous. Current thinking is that this expansion of Lapita people out of Near Oceania happened very rapidly. One or two hundred years may have been all it took.

Becoming Polynesian

A glance at the map (pages 16-17) shows that the Fiji group is most likely to have been the point of first landfall across the ocean from the west. The settlement of Fiji about 3000 years ago was followed closely by that of Tonga and Samoa. In all three island groups the earliest settlements are identified by decorated and plain Lapita pottery, at the eastern end of its geographical range. The distinctive Polynesian way of life developed out of the older Lapita culture.

At first, contact may have been maintained between the scattered settlements by regular canoe voyaging, which also maintained contact to and from Melanesian islands to the west. As populations grew, however, communities would have come to depend less on

Stone head of a tiki figure from the Marquesas Islands, East Polynesia. Ht 420 mm. (Auckland Museum 50690)

external contacts and more on the social and economic resources of their home islands. Changes in language and culture then began to distinguish the different island peoples. It was a process that was repeated many times in the course of peopling the Pacific.

Some time after colonisation of the region there was a division between early Fijian and Polynesian languages, which distinguishes the two language groups and peoples to this day. Subsequently, there was a split between Tongan and Samoan branches of 'Proto-Polynesian'. Linguists label the early Polynesian languages 'Proto-Tongic' and 'Proto-Nuclear Polynesian'.

Languages descended from the former are Tongan, Niuean and Uvean, while it is likely that all other Polynesian languages are descended from the early form spoken in Samoa. Thus the further expansion of people to the east was from the region of Samoa, or from nearby islands such as Tokelau, where the language was also

The Hawaiian lei niho palaoa *was developed from the ancient imitation whale tooth form found throughout Polynesia. Braided cords are of human hair.* (Auckland Museum 14537)

From Asia to Aotearoa: peopling the Pacific

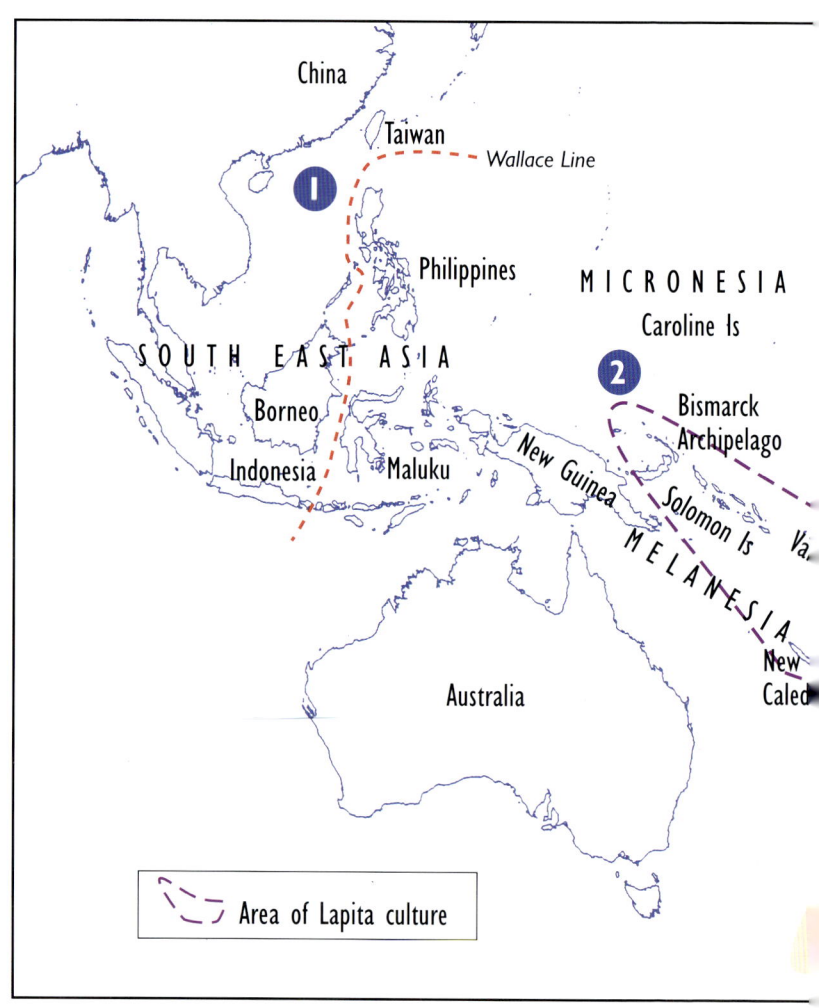

1. *5000 years ago: Austronesian-speaking ancestors of Polynesian and other Pacific peoples move south from Taiwan and South China into the vast archipelago of island Southeast Asia.*

2. *3500 years ago: they reach the Bismarck group, east of New Guinea. These people are skilled sailors, and are known by their 'Lapita' pottery, a name now given to the culture and people.*

3. *3000 years ago: Lapita people are the first to discover and settle the island groups of Vanuatu, New Caledonia, Fiji, Tonga and Samoa.*

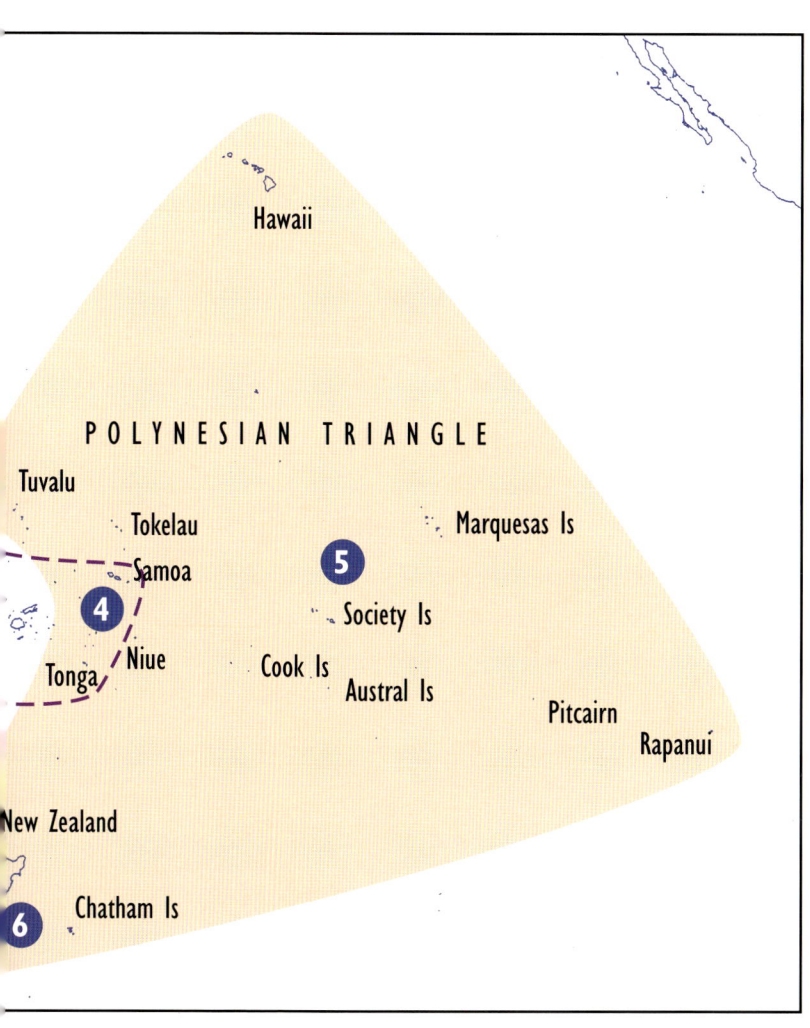

4. Polynesian culture and language develop in Tonga and Samoa and nearby island groups.

5. 1500-1000 years ago: people settle the island groups of East Polynesia – the Cooks, Societies, Marquesas, Hawaii and Rapanui.

6. 700-800 years ago: Aotearoa is the last Pacific archipelago to be discovered and settled by Polynesian people, who develop here the unique Maori way of life.

derived from Proto-Nuclear Polynesian. But it is not at all clear just when people moved on from West Polynesia (that is, Samoa, Tonga and neighbouring islands) to the tiny islands further east. Most archaeologists agree there was a pause in the settlement of Polynesia at this stage; but was it 500 years – or as much as 1500 years? The first good evidence for settlement in the Southern Cooks and the Society Islands, at the geographic heart of East Polynesia, is in the period 800-1000 AD.

If the above dates do indeed reflect first settlement of the island groups, why did it take so long for such experienced voyagers to move on from West Polynesia? Was there a period between discovery and settlement? Also, if settlement was so late, where and when did the distinctive aspects of Eastern Polynesian culture emerge? Are we arguing here for hundreds of years of isolation for such a cultural development, or for rapid change when a small number of people first arrived in a new and isolated environment?

The location and timing of any prolonged development of Eastern Polynesian culture has yet to be identified by archaeology. Alternatively, rapid change may have been the result of some sort of 'founder effect' – by which only part of the original culture makes it to the new land. Another possibility is that the limited resources of atolls in particular, and the small high islands of the central and east Pacific, reduced options and demanded rapid change, thus hastening the development of distinctive aspects of Eastern Polynesian culture.

The Eastern Polynesian cultural complex includes new

Moai kavakava *figure, Rapanui (Easter Island). 400 mm. At the remote southeast corner of the Polynesian triangle, Rapanui is best known for its huge stone sculptures. (Auckland Museum 2751)

forms of fishing gear and stone adzes, and a range of personal ornaments made of ivory, bone and shell. All are found in early settlements in New Zealand. Not seen here is the elaborate stone-built religious marae, which may have developed in central East Polynesia after New Zealand was settled. Subsistence depended on the domesticated animals and food plants brought from the west, and exploitation of the marine resources of reefs and open seas.

Pottery, which had been made by ancestors of Polynesians for thousands of years, was not made on the atolls and high islands of East Polynesia where there is no clay. By the time people reached New Zealand, where there is clay in abundance, the ancient craft was lost. Without pottery, Maori and other Polynesians cook their food in umu or hangi (earth ovens). These were used by pre-Lapita people in the western Pacific, and are also found, along with pottery, in ancient Lapita sites.

Whatever the course and timing of settlement, it is clear that by the end of the first millennium AD people were living throughout central East Polynesia, including the Cooks, Societies, Australs, Tuamotu and Marquesas island groups. At first, as in the western Pacific hundreds of years earlier, a small and scattered population may have been held together by regular canoe voyaging. Later, as island communities grew to self-sufficiency, communication with distant islands became intermittent, or was lost altogether.

This process may be illustrated by the so-called 'mystery islands' of the Pacific, which have evidence of people once having lived on them, but which were abandoned before European voyagers first came across them in the 18th or 19th century. There are nearly 30 of them, all small and isolated, and many of them on ocean routes between larger islands or archipelagoes. Archaeologist Geoffrey Irwin argues that they were occupied as long as there was regular voyaging, but that the isolated islands proved too small to sustain a population once contact with other communities became irregular or ceased.

The voyage

The evidence of material culture, language, cultivated food plants and human biology all point to the first New Zealanders having come from somewhere in central East Polynesia. The most likely points of departure are the Society, Cook or Austral Islands, with the more distant Tuamotu and Marquesas groups, even Mangareva

Necklace of whale tooth ivory, sennit fibre and human hair from Rurutu, Austral Islands. The Australs are among the closest East Polynesian islands to Aotearoa. (Auckland Museum 31491)

or Pitcairn, also being possibilities. It is unlikely there was only one island of origin: once sailing directions were known, settlement canoes may have left a number of islands, over a period of years – or even generations.

The discovery and settlement of Aotearoa depended on the voyaging skills of Polynesian people. As we have seen, the vessels and seamanship needed were first developed among the islands of Southeast Asia and Melanesia. In the Pacific Ocean, new skills and navigational knowledge were needed for much longer voyages. There is a huge difference between sailing over an enclosed sea to an island visible from the point of departure, and sailing for thousands of kilometres over open ocean.

But why did our first settlers come from more than 3000 km away in East Polynesia, and not from New Caledonia or Fiji, which are little more than half that distance from North Cape – and which have been occupied for 3000 years? In answering this, it must first be remembered that even North Cape, the northernmost part of

New Zealand, is much further from the equator than any other Polynesian island, and so lay outside the regularly traversed tropical ocean of ancient voyagers. Quite simply, New Zealand was very hard to find.

The strategy of exploration voyages may also be significant. For many years it was thought that the first discoverers of remote Pacific islands used the wind behind them to sail out into the unknown. Geoffrey Irwin, however, has argued that Polynesian explorers are more likely to have sailed upwind, to retain the option of running for home, should nothing be found. Hence, the discovery of Aotearoa had to wait for settlement far to the east, before explorers could confidently enter the south-west Pacific into the reliable westerly winds of temperate latitudes.

The discovery and settlement of New Zealand may have taken place in that period of regular voyaging, which for some time kept up contact between the scattered early communities of central East Polynesia. Voyages both ways are recorded in Maori tradition. Thus, Aotearoa may have been, for an unknown time, part of a wider Eastern Polynesian voyaging community. At the time New Zealand was settled, there also took place the discovery and settlement of nearby 'mystery islands', Norfolk and Raoul Island, which were occupied, but then abandoned as regular voyaging in the south-west Pacific came to an end.

The vessels used are likely to have been double-hulled canoes – that is, with two hulls joined by a living platform. Such craft are fast and stable, and had the carrying capacity necessary for

Raoul Island in the Kermadec Group is a 'mystery island', abandoned before Europeans first visited in the late 18th century. Evidence of its former inhabitants includes the Pacific cabbage tree, ti pore, pictured at Denham Bay, which was taken throughout the Pacific by early Polynesians as a valued food source.

Food pounders for mashing taro and breadfruit were used throughout East Polynesia, but not by Maori, suggesting that they were developed in central East Polynesia after the settlement of New Zealand. Tahiti; Ht 160 mm. (Auckland Museum 19501.3)

settlement voyages. It is possible that smaller outrigger canoes were also used. Voyaging canoes might carry 10-30 people, depending on the anticipated length of the voyage, the necessary cargo of tools and equipment, animals and plants, and the size of the vessel.

In late 1985, 'Hawaiki-nui', a 20-m long double-hulled canoe made of traditional materials, sailed from Rarotonga in the southern Cook Islands to Motiti Island near Tauranga, in 22 days, using traditional navigation skills and sailing instructions. 'Hokule'a', a 19-m canoe from Hawai'i, made a 17 days' passage from Rarotonga to the Bay of Islands at the same time.

The people who travelled here on their ocean-going canoes brought with them the language, religious beliefs, knowledge and experience of their forebears. They may also have had a greater spirit of adventure than those they left behind, since it was they who left a loved and well-known homeland. Such an element in their make-up would have served them well on the voyage, and when they arrived in a land so different to all their previous experience.

Dating the first settlement

In the 1970s, when the writer was a student at Otago University, there was wide agreement among archaeologists that New Zealand was first settled in the 10th century (900-1000 AD), or perhaps a little before. This settlement date had a long history, which archaeological work at the time, and radiocarbon dating in particular, seemed to confirm.

Its origin was research into Maori accounts of settlement voyages, mostly carried out a century or more ago by Pakeha scholars. In this research, Maori voyaging traditions were searched for matching stories, and the genealogies counted back to establish a date, given an average number of years per generation.

It was this method which gave the dates known by generations of New Zealanders: 950 AD for the voyage of discovery by Kupe, 1150 AD for a voyage by Toi, and 1350 AD for the so-called 'Great Fleet'. In his 1976 book, *The Great New Zealand Myth*, David Simmons showed this story to be seriously flawed, not least because it tried to make a single narrative out of many different tribal accounts.

Nonetheless, radiocarbon dates did seem to support first settlement in the 10th century, despite the fact that sites dated to the 10th century itself were proving hard to find. There were many 11th- and 12th-century sites, especially on the east coasts of both islands, and it was argued that since some generations would have been needed for such widespread occupation to become established, the 10th century might be about right. Examples of the very few settlements dating from the first one or two hundred years of people living in New Zealand would eventually be located.

A quarter of a century on, the early sites still have not been found. In the meantime, more has been learned of the technical difficulties of radiocarbon dating, so that the once accepted 11th- and 12th-century dates are seen now as highly problematic. As an example, charcoal from long-lived tree species dates the growth of the timber, and not when it was burned in a settlement cooking fire, so that radiocarbon dates from unidentified charcoals are therefore

A coconut grove on Rarotonga, Cook Islands, 1903. Rarotonga is a likely departure point for settlement canoes leaving for Aotearoa. (Henry Winkelmann, Gudgeon Album, Auckland Museum W115)

suspect. Wood identification was not routinely carried out in the early years of radiocarbon dating.

In 1991, New Zealand archaeologist Atholl Anderson looked at all radiocarbon dates which cast light on the matter of first settlement, and concluded that no acceptable date before the 12th century could be found for any early settlement site. He went on to argue that since the dated sites include some which show every likelihood of being early in the settlement of New Zealand, we should look to this direct archaeological evidence, rather than indications of secondary environmental impacts, for the date of first settlement. Early sites are identified by their Eastern Polynesian artefact types, and by the bones of moa and other birds which were soon extinct following human settlement.

Since then, new work has been carried out on dating the important Wairau Bar site in Marlborough. The kinds of artefacts found at the site suggest it was first occupied early in the settlement history of New Zealand. Indeed, it is quite possible that the first people living at Wairau Bar were first generation settlers, who made the canoe voyage from East Polynesia.

Fourteen new radiocarbon dates on moa egg shell and cockle

shell, along with a reassessment of dates previously obtained, point to occupation of Wairau Bar late in the 13th century.

At the same time, different ways of establishing a date of first settlement are offered by new lines of environmental enquiry. Important among these are the presence in New Zealand of kiore (or Pacific rat), which could only have been transported here by people, and environmental impacts suggesting human intervention, which can be traced by pollen studies and other signs of environmental change.

The most important environmental indicator of first settlement relates to vegetation change brought about by human activity. As soon as they arrived, people began clearing forest, whether for gardens or hunting game or other reasons. This is reflected in plant pollens found at different levels in swamp deposits according to age, the deepest samples being the oldest. Pollen studies throughout New Zealand show a change from forest species to bracken fern and other plants of the open country. The change can be dated by the radiocarbon method.

There have been claims that pollen and other indicators of environmental change show human impacts well before the oldest dated settlement sites. But there are alternative explanations, such as natural fires or local environmental changes, for what can be difficult evidence – compounded by the problems of obtaining accurate radiocarbon dates from swamp deposits. A recent study by pollen scientists Matt McGlone and Janet Wilmshurst concludes that there is no good pollen evidence for human-induced environmental change prior to the 13th century.

In recent years a great deal of interest and controversy have been generated by suggestions that kiore have been in New Zealand for as much as 2000 years. It is not claimed there was human settlement at such an early date, although kiore can only have come in company with humans. Instead, it is being suggested that a canoe – or canoes – reached New Zealand, leaving kiore behind on both main islands, but no permanent human settlement.

The idea that kiore have been here for so long again depends on radiocarbon dates, and there has been a lot of debate on problems related to the dating of kiore bone. The issues are of a technical nature, concerning the way bone is prepared for analysis, and the possible effects of rat diet or contamination of bone by ancient carbon. Meanwhile, the early dates have not been confirmed by field evidence.

A whalebone club from Huahine, one of the Society Islands, dates from about the time New Zealand was first settled. The similarity to Maori patu is part of evidence for our first settlers having come from central East Polynesia. 370 mm. (Auckland Museum – cast 48060)

If kiore did reach New Zealand centuries before human settlement, the implications are quite fascinating for our human and natural history. But it is surprising that such a cataclysmic event for the isolated and vulnerable New Zealand fauna has not proved easier to confirm. Also, DNA analysis shows that New Zealand kiore are from East Polynesia. They cannot, therefore, have arrived here before people (and rats) reached that part of the Pacific – and it is by no means certain that that was as early as 2000 years ago. The jury is out on the subject of early kiore.

A conclusion based on current evidence is that the first settlement canoes hauled up on a beach, probably on the east coast of the North Island, some time in the 13th century – or perhaps the 12th century. As more work is carried out, a radical revision of the date becomes less likely, but the fate of the old consensus for a 10th century date shows us that widely held views can always be overturned by tomorrow's new discovery.

What else was in the canoes?

The people from East Polynesia who were to become the first New Zealanders were the inheritors of hundreds of years of experience in the settlement of Pacific islands. They understood the preparation and strategy needed for a successful settlement voyage, and they knew what they needed to take with them. Voyaging canoes would have been carefully loaded with tools and equipment, and the familiar plants and animals that had been part of a traditional way of life for thousands of years.

We have seen that the Southeast Asian ancestors of Polynesians possessed the pig, dog and chicken. These animals were domesticated before 2000 BC, and accompanied people on their odyssey into the Pacific. Also transported on voyaging canoes throughout Remote Oceania was the Pacific rat, or kiore. Like the other animals, kiore originated in Southeast Asia, but whether it was a stowaway or deliberately transported is not clear.

All four animals accompanied people throughout most of the Pacific, the bones of pig, chicken, dog and kiore being found in pre-European settlement sites in the western Pacific, and in central East Polynesia – including the Cook, Society and Marquesas groups. All of the domesticated animals were also successfully introduced into the Hawaiian Islands, at the distant northern corner of the Polynesian Triangle. But, only the chicken (and kiore) reached Rapanui (Easter Island) in the far south-east, and only the dog (and kiore) reached – or survived in – Aotearoa.

It is a reasonable assumption that settlement voyages set out with all the Polynesian domesticated animals, since all were important in the traditional way of life. That only the dog was successfully introduced into New Zealand may reflect on the rigours of the voyage (the other animals died or were eaten on the way), and also, perhaps, on just how few voyages there were. There may have been few chances for the animals to make it, compared to other destinations. Not one of the domesticated animals reached the Chatham Islands, the people who settled there being accompanied only by that most successful of Pacific fellow travellers, the kiore.

Like the animals, most Pacific food plants originated in Southeast Asia, or New Guinea, where their wild progenitors grow; although there is an intriguing exception, to which we shall return in a moment. Important among plants brought into the Pacific from the west are taro, yam, banana, breadfruit and coconut. All are tropical plants, and some of them, even if they made it to New Zealand on settlement canoes, did not survive in our temperate climate.

Maori ancestors successfully introduced into New Zealand the food plants, taro, yam (uwhi), gourd (hue) and kumara. The first three came from the west, although the gourd is also known from the ancient Americas. Maori were thus heirs of the ancient Southeast Asian domestication and development of root crops.

Kumara, however, originated in the Americas, and probably entered the Pacific from the region of Peru. Just how is a matter for speculation: Thor Heyerdahl's famous 1947 voyage on a balsawood raft from Peru to the Tuamotu Islands suggests one way it may have happened. But it would seem more likely that Polynesians, who were the great voyagers of the Pacific, made it to South America and returned to East Polynesia with tubers or plants. As a root crop grown for its tubers, kumara would have been readily adopted by Pacific people with long experience of similar plants.

Other plants introduced by our first settlers are the aute or paper mulberry (*Broussonetia papyrifera*), and ti pore or Pacific cabbage tree (*Cordyline terminalis*). Both are likely to have originated in Southeast Asia, and are found in Melanesia, and throughout the Pacific to the furthest corners of the Polynesian Triangle. Aute was used for making tapa cloth, and survived here until the late 18th century, when Joseph Banks saw it growing at the Bay of Islands. Ti was grown for its massive root, which produced a large quantity of sugary starch when cooked in an earth oven (umu ti).

Tapa beater from a streambed at Aka Aka, South Auckland. The Asian aute (paper mulberry) tree was introduced by our first settlers, and was used in the north for making tapa until the 18th century. 310 mm. (Auckland Museum 36234)

A fishing lure shank made of pearl shell found at Tairua, Coromandel Peninsula, was brought here from the tropical Pacific on an ancient voyaging canoe; the shell does not occur naturally in New Zealand. 50 mm. (Auckland Museum AU1785)

As well as animals and food plants, settlement canoes would have contained a variety of tools, implements, weapons, and personal clothes and ornaments which were particularly valued, or just plain useful, or both. Setting up in a new land would require fishing gear, wood-working tools, and implements for gardening, hunting and food preparation. The kinds of personal ornaments brought by the first settlers are outlined in another book in this series, *Nga Tohu Tawhito: early Maori ornaments*.

In the Auckland War Memorial Museum is the only known item which safely can be argued to have come to New Zealand from East Polynesia on an ancient voyaging canoe. A fishing lure shank found at Tairua on the Coromandel Peninsula's east coast is made of tropical black-lipped pearl shell (*Pteria magaritifera*), which does not occur naturally here. It was recovered in the course of an archaeological excavation, so that radiocarbon dating has been possible, giving a date for the lure – and settlement – of the late 13th to mid-14th century AD.

Was there anyone else?

There is a long history of weird and wonderful speculation on the subject of ancient arrivals in New Zealand. Newspapers and other media regularly pick up stories of fantastic claims relating to ancient Egyptians, Phoenicians and Libyans, supposed early Celtic settlement in the north, or to curiosities like the 'Kaimanawa Wall', and strange artefacts supposed to have been left by ancient pre-Maori peoples. Still more fanciful are claims of vanished continents or visitors from space.

Many New Zealanders believe there was a pre-Maori race in this country, known as 'Moriori'. There is a lot of confusion about this. Moriori are a Polynesian people who have lived on the Chatham Islands for hundreds of years. They probably went there from New Zealand, their founding ancestors therefore being the same early Maori people who were living in New Zealand at the time. Alternatively, but less likely, the islands may have been discovered and settled directly from East Polynesia.

It was in the isolated Chatham Islands that the Moriori people developed their unique attributes of language, culture and way of life. Moriori themselves did not live in New Zealand, or in East Polynesia, any more than it can be said that the people who came here from England in the 19th century were Pakeha New Zealanders before they set out.

The term 'Moa-hunter' is also sometimes used for supposed pre-Maori inhabitants of New Zealand. Again, this is based on a simple confusion. The hunters of the giant flightless moa were the first Polynesian settlers of Aotearoa, who were the ancestors of the Maori. At that time their way of life was, of course, very different to that of their Maori descendants, and their distinctive tools and ornaments were more like older Polynesian forms, but they were not a different people.

There is no good evidence of anyone, other than that branch of Polynesian people now known as Maori, ever having lived in New Zealand prior to the arrival of Europeans at the end of the 18th century. Any other suggestion, for example of Viking burials on Auckland's North Shore, or a peaceful pre-Maori 'Waitaha' people, or Egyptians or Celts or others, is wishful thinking and invention.

Becoming Maori

The first settlers who arrived in New Zealand some time in the 13th century possessed the same knowledge, language, technical skills and life experience – in short, culture – as people of the East Polynesian Pacific islands they left behind. It could not be otherwise, since prior to their arrival their lives had been lived elsewhere. It was in New Zealand that the Polynesian people who came here became Maori.

Becoming Maori involved a developing relationship with an environment that was entirely new in the Polynesian experience. Here for the first time, Polynesians from small tropical high islands and atolls encountered estuaries, rivers and lakes, huge forests and giant timber trees, inland mountains and plains, cold winters and a brief growing season for food crops.

There were new rocks requiring new techniques for crafting into stone tools, weapons and ornaments, and a multitude of new plants and animals to learn about, which could be used for many different purposes. Fearless birds – many without the power of flight – were easy prey; seals on the beaches and headlands offered a new and rich source of food; techniques were developed for making clothes from previously unknown plants such as harakeke (flax).

For thousands of years, Polynesian and earlier ancestors of Maori lived in and understood the world of tropical Asia and the Pacific. Their way of life was adapted to a tropical climate and seas, to tropical plants and animals, and to the year-round gardening of food crops. The first New Zealanders were faced with an enormous challenge of learning about a strange new temperate land and its resources, and creating here a new way of life based on their Polynesian cultural heritage. How the people did this, and transformed themselves into the Maori of Aotearoa, is another story.

Acknowledgements and further reading

I would like to thank Atholl Anderson, Ross Clark, Janet Davidson, Jeff Evans, Louise Furey, Roger Green, Tom Higham, Richard Holdaway, Geoff Irwin, Lisa Matisoo-Smith, Matt McGlone, Reg Nichol, Kath Prickett, Paul Tapsell and Richard Walter for references and discussion on different issues. Thanks also to Andrew Mayo for his help with the photography.

The following references include books and articles mentioned in the text.

Anderson, Atholl, 1991. The chronology of colonization in New Zealand. *Antiquity* Vol. 65, pp. 767-797.

Bellwood, Peter, 1978. *Man's Conquest of the Pacific*. Collins, Auckland.

Blust, Robert, 1995. The prehistory of the Austronesian-speaking peoples: a view from language. *Journal of World Prehistory* Vol. 9, pp. 453-510.

Davidson, Janet, 1984. *The Prehistory of New Zealand*. Auckland, Longman Paul.

Higham, Thomas, Atholl Anderson and Chris Jacomb, 1999. Dating the first New Zealanders: the chronology of Wairau Bar. *Antiquity* Vol 73, pp. 420-427.

Irwin, Geoffrey, 1992. *The Prehistoric Exploration and Colonisation of the Pacific*. Cambridge (England), Cambridge University Press.

Kirch, Patrick Vinton, 1997. *The Lapita Peoples: ancestors of the oceanic world*. Cambridge (Massachusetts), Blackwell.

McGlone, Matt and Janet Wilmshurst, 1999. Dating initial Maori environmental impact in New Zealand. *Quaternary International* Vol. 59, pp. 5-16.

Simmons, David, 1976. *The Great New Zealand Myth*. Wellington, Reed.

Sutton, Douglas (ed.), 1994. *The Origins of the First New Zealanders*. Auckland, Auckland University Press.

First published in 2001 by
David Bateman Ltd, 30 Tarndale Grove,
Albany, Auckland, New Zealand

in association with Auckland War Memorial Museum

Copyright © Auckland War Memorial Museum, 2001
Copyright © David Bateman Ltd, 2001
Reprinted 2004

ISBN 1 86953 463 8

This book is copyright. Except for the purpose of fair review, no part may be stored or transmitted in any form or by any means, electronic or mechanical, including recording or storage in any information retrieval systems, without permission in writing from the publishers. No reproduction may be made, whether by photocopying or by any other means, unless a licence has been obtained from the publisher or its agent.

Design by ExPress Communications Ltd
Printed in China through Colorcraft Ltd., HK